INSPIRATIONAL IDEAS FOR
Embroidery
ON CLOTHES & ACCESSORIES

Thank you very much to all of the embroiderers
who have allowed us to photograph their work for
this book. I am sure that your creativity will be a
great inspiration to others.

INSPIRATIONAL IDEAS FOR
Embroidery
ON CLOTHES & ACCESSORIES

GAIL LAWTHER

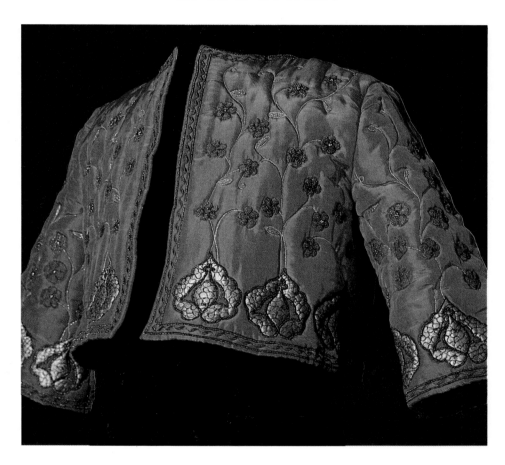

SEARCH PRESS

First published in Great Britain 1993
Search Press Limited, Wellwood, North Farm Road, Tunbridge
Wells, Kent TN2 3DR

Text, illustrations, and photographs copyright © 1993 Search
Press Limited

All photographs by Search Press Studios, with the exception of
those on pages 55 (top left, top right, bottom right) and 79 by
Christopher Lawther, and those on page 55 (centre, bottom
left) by Caroline Calder.

ISBN 0 85532 711 1

Printed in Singapore by
Huntsmen Offset Printing Pte Ltd

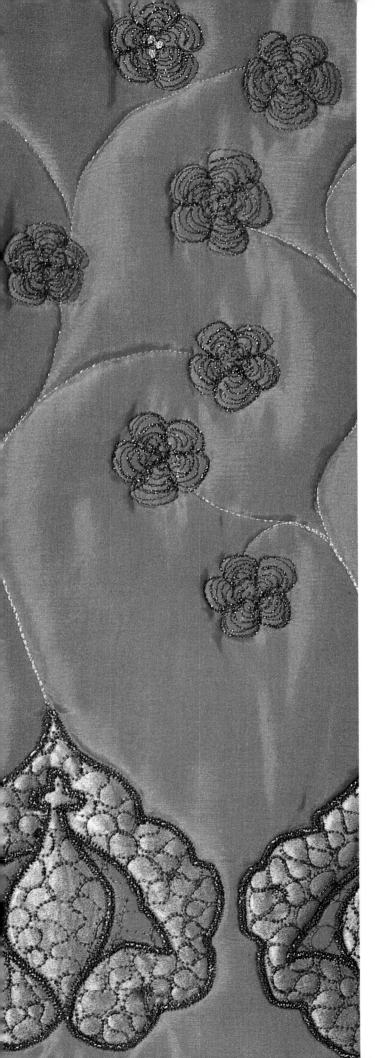

CONTENTS

INTRODUCTION

Wearable art is the phrase that describes the contents of this book! Clothes have always been a way of expressing individuality, and that is even more the case if the wearer has designed, made and embellished the garment or accessory herself. Embroidery is so much more than just stitching around the lines of a transfer pattern. It is a chance to experiment with colour, texture, stitchery, and all kinds of exciting techniques.

I have chosen all of the items in this book for their inspirational quality. Most of them have taken many hours of work, and all of them are unique works of art. Also, I have deliberately included widely varying techniques and approaches. Some of the pieces are based on relatively straightforward ideas, whilst others are almost unbelievable in their complexity. However, they all reflect the one idea that there is no limit as to how far you can take embroidered fashion.

The creativity and imagination of these designers are breath-taking, from the one who has based a slipper design on the silvery scales of a cobra, to the one who has created a gorgeous wedding dress inspired by the tree of life motif. The originality of some of the techniques used is awesome too. One designer has burned holes in a fabric with an incense stick, one has made her own scarab fastening for an Egyptian necklace, whilst several others have machined layers of fabric together and torn or cut them back to different depths.

If you have ever worked through your own embroidery designs, then you will know that some ideas just fall into place virtually straight-away, whilst others have to go through many reworkings and trials before they look just right. When I was collecting material for this book, I asked each designer to give me some insights into how they arrived at their finished design. They have allowed their trial pieces, inspirational items and sketch-books to be photographed, and have talked honestly about ideas that worked and ideas that did not. Their inspirational sources vary from the mundane to the exotic, from a broken railing or a begonia to the gold of the Pharaohs or the colours of Guatemalan weaving. The variety of techniques that they have used is an inspiration in itself. Several of the designers have made their own fabrics, by felting fibres, by stitching together snippets of other fabrics, or by working intricate stitchery on a special dissolvable fabric which disappears when it is ironed or dipped into water. The embroiderers have incorporated beads, sequins, braids, ribbons, buttons, and found objects, and have worked on every fabric from the sheerest voile to the thickest leather.

The embroidery shown in the book represents the work of designers of all levels of experience, from young college students to people who have been embroidering for many decades. Some of them are professionals, but many of the designers simply embroider as a hobby, because it is so satisfying. I hope that you will find this book an inspiration, and that all the design ideas and techniques will encourage you to create your own wearable art.

A sample from Adele Dargue's collection 'Putting on the Glitz' (see pages 28-31).

Colour

INSPIRATION FROM COLOUR

To the embroiderer, colour is a vital tool. Many people just take colour for granted, or simply do not realize its effect, but if you have an artistic eye then you will find that you automatically use colour well, whether that is in your embroidery, when you paint your living room, or in the clothes that you choose to wear. Of course, this does not mean that the colours you use always have to have a bland harmony about them; strong, deliberate clashes can be as effective in embroidery as they can be in music or architecture.

When you are looking for inspiration, you will be looking at the colours of things even when you do not realize it. Your brain will be thinking things like 'that is an interesting mixture of colours', or 'I think that green is too dominant', or 'what a striking combination'. Also, when you remember a scene, you will tend to remember the colours that were linked with it and the sensations that they produced in you.

There is a kind of symbolism associated with colour too, different colours conjuring up different associations in our minds. White is still traditionally associated with purity, but also has an airy, or ethereal, quality. Black is associated with darkness, and also with mystery and the exotic. Gold represents opulence in many people's minds, and red, purple, emerald, and rich blue are royal colours. Pastel shades evoke delicacy, innocence, childhood, and pretty country flowers, whilst strong colours provide images of tribal art, tropical countries, and bright sunlit days. Greys and silvers make us think of winter, green and red together suggest Christmas, and browns, beiges, and gold conjure up autumn. Colours can also provoke emotions. Close harmonies are restful, clashes make us sit up and take notice, neutral colours blend into the background, and fluorescent colours are disturbing to the eye – and the brain!

All of these ideas make rich hunting grounds for embroiderers. Try different ideas in your mind, and see what colours come to your thoughts to represent them. For instance, what colour schemes come to mind for the following ideas – kingfisher, party, pebbles, baby, old people's home, classical concert, cottage garden, Japan, space travel, fairground, Antarctic, wedding feast, harvest festival? Think up some other ideas and jot down colour schemes for them. Can you think up alternative schemes for any of them? For instance, the colours for a party are likely to be different if you are thinking about a child's birthday party than if you are thinking about a moonlit beach party.

If you are not used to being inspired by colours themselves, then try using the photographs on the opposite page as starting points for your own ideas. Also, try interpreting the same basic colour scheme in different media. Coloured pencils will give a very different effect from felt-tipped pens, or from fabric paints on a piece of muslin, or from snippets of coloured paper cut from magazines. In this section of the book, all of the items have been inspired by colour in different forms. These range from bright jewels and stained glass windows to the colours of jungle paintings and experiments with the primary colours. They provide a visual feast, and will give you plenty of ideas for taking your own colour experiments further!

STAINED GLASS SHIRT

Designed by Tara Mann

Tara lives fairly near Canterbury, and the stained glass windows in the cathedral there, along with the stained glass art of other cathedrals, provided much of the inspiration for her collection of menswear. She says, 'I have always been fascinated by the richness and colour of stained glass, and by its illuminated effects. Medieval stained glass seemed easier to reproduce than that of other periods because of its mosaic construction. When I was tackling the construction problem as it might relate to a garment, I visited a friend's brother who is a stained glass artist. He showed me the appropriate places where the glass would have to be cut and where the leading would need to be placed. In my collection, I used pure cottons and cotton organza for a sheer effect. Originally, I had wanted to use silk organza for greater drama, but it was too expensive.' For her shirt, Tara appliquéd the fabrics to the background first, then worked the leading between the coloured areas in black cord and machine embroidery.

Tara decided to work on a range of clothes for men as she feels that they have been neglected in the history of fashion. 'Women have always been the decorated race, so I decided to turn my attention to men. I think that there is a gap in the market for one-off men's garments featuring surface decoration, and for clothes that allow a bit of exhibitionism.'

Shirt and jacket designs from Tara's 'stained glass' collection of menswear.

ITALIAN STYLE TOP

SHIRT WITH BORDED CIRCLE

CANVASWORK WAISTCOAT
Designed by Esme Wagstaffe

Esme enjoys the discipline of working on canvas and feels that within its limits there is great scope for creativity. At the time that she began the waistcoat, she was teaching dressmaking in an open prison. She says, 'One of the girls had started a very imaginative embroidered waistcoat, and this inspired another girl, an American, to make one for her boyfriend back home – it was a magnificent design of fields, mountains, skyscraper and sunset. I brought both of these works home to block into shape and they were greatly admired. My son decided that a really satisfying eighteenth birthday present would be an equally original and exclusive waistcoat. I suggested several pictorial designs but these were eventually rejected in favour of a quieter geometric design.'

Esme took the pattern from a favourite waistcoat and simplified it, making up a toile to check the fit. She marked the pattern shapes on to the canvas with a line of watercolour, and stretched the canvas in a frame whilst she worked on it. She stitched almost exclusively in a simplified Florentine, or Bargello, pattern, and the design just grew from the colours themselves. 'Whilst I was making it, I went to a lecture by Kaffe Fassett, who surprised many members of his audience by saying that he often adjusted colours and shapes as his work went along. I was delighted. So many designers seem to know exactly what the end result will be before they start. Not me!'

When the embroidery was finished, she cut out the back and lining in satin and made up the waistcoat by machine, finishing the seams by hand-whipping red silk over the top stitching. As a final touch, she made Somerset buttons by hand, to match the waistcoat colours. Her son enjoyed wearing an embroidered pattern which he felt sure was based on W for Wagstaffe!

PRIMARY JACKET
Designed by Susan Fraser

Susan's jacket design began as an exercise in colour and line. Her first task was to cover sheets of paper with circles or arcs, which were drawn in different media to give different textures and densities. Then, she repeated the same idea using colour. Susan deliberately limited herself to the primary colours for this project. She had spent the previous six months creating a large machine-embroidered wall-hanging, using sixty-eight different shades of blue thread to create subtle blends of colour, and she was now interested to see what effects she could get by using and overlapping the three bright colours.

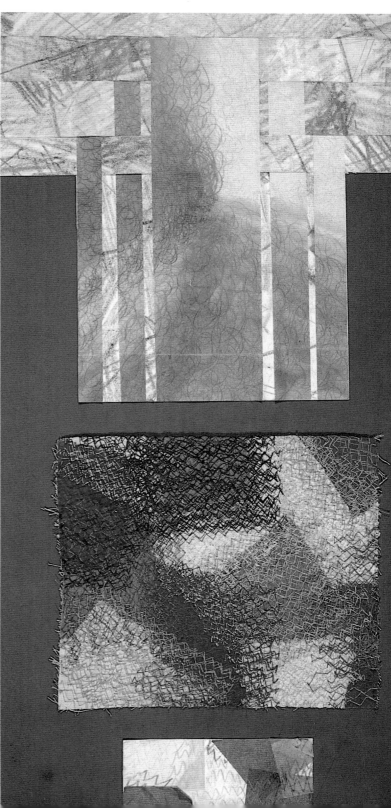

For the foundation of the jacket, Susan used red, yellow, and blue cotton fabrics cut into random-sized squares. Then, she zigzag-stitched over them in primary-coloured threads to create a variety of textures and to blend the colours of the background fabrics. The back of the jacket was completely covered in stitchery, mostly whip-stitch, and this section alone took about forty hours of machine stitching! The underarm seams of the sleeves were stitched conventionally, but other seams were worked by laying more squares of fabric across them and adding extra embroidery. Susan left the inside of the jacket unlined; she had deliberately used six different shades of blue bobbin thread so that they would create their own texture and subtle colour blends.

As Susan's main aim was to create a garment with a stunning colour impact, she kept the shape of the jacket itself very simple.

PARROT WAISTCOAT

Designed by Anita Faithful

'A great many influences prompt me to make my jackets and waistcoats. The original inspiration for this garment came from the jungle paintings of Henri Rousseau, and then from seeing the lush pictures by Marion North at Kew Gardens. I often sketch and design on wallpaper lining paper, as it is the right width for most pattern pieces and very cheap and easy to obtain!'

Anita draws her designs on to the lining paper and, once she is satisfied, outlines it in very black pen or pencil so that she can trace it on to the background fabric. She uses a medium-weight silk habutai, pre-washed and ironed to remove any dressing. Once the design has been traced lightly in soft pencil, she stretches the silk across a frame to keep it taut whilst she applies gutta resist – this creates a dye-proof barrier in the same way that batik uses barriers of wax. She uses very intense silk dyes, then steams the fabric to fix the dyes and make them washable.

For this particular waistcoat, Anita placed the silk on to a layer of 50g (2oz) polyester wadding and a layer of butter muslin, then machine-quilted the design with a narrow satin stitch in rayon thread, covering all the lines left by the gutta. Once the quilting was complete, she cut out the pattern pieces and assembled the waistcoat, piped the edges, and lined it with a contrasting colour of lightweight habutai.

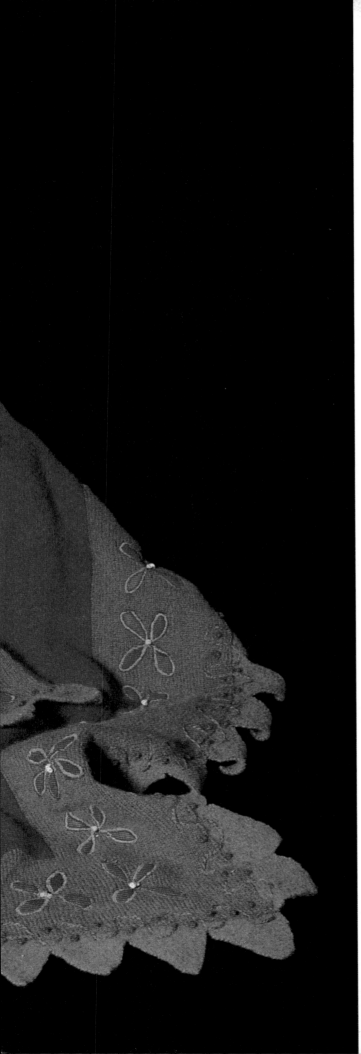

FELTED WRAP AND HAT

Designed by Louise Mills

Louise created a collection of felted wraps and hats for her final college project. All of her work was based on the arts and crafts of Guatemala, and Gianni Vecchiato's book *Guatemalan Rainbow* was her main source of inspiration. The people of Guatemala are poor in materialistic terms but rich in the beauty of the clothes that they wear, and Louise aimed to re-create this richness by using coloured wools and intricate embroidery. All of the basic knitting was done on an electronic knitting machine using four-ply lamb's-wool. She wanted the items to feel soft, so she felted them by putting them through the hot cycle in a washing machine – this makes the fibres lock together. For the wrap, she knitted and felted a separate green strip of the same length; because the felting process stops the knitted fabric from fraying, she could then cut the zigzag border and join it to the wrap with a special linking machine.

For the embroidery, Louise machine-appliquéd simple irregular pink felt flower shapes, adding touches of hand embroidery in the chunky French knots which she worked in red, blue, and yellow. The hat was decorated in the same way, with the addition of tiny hearts and purple and turquoise wool circles around the flowers, plus machine-appliquéd swirls of wool as an embroidered border.

EVENING BAG

Designed by Pat Wilkins

A drawing of a broken ear-ring was the inspiration for this beautiful evening bag, the shape of which reflects the sharp geometric shapes of cut or broken glass. When Pat designed it, she was also exploring the design possibilities of art jewellery and glass!

She wanted a firm, closely woven fabric for the background, preferably with a sheen to reproduce the glitter and gleam of glass, so she chose a gun-metal grey taffeta embossed with lines of machine embroidery in a metallic thread. She used brightly coloured areas of blended machine stitching to emboss the background fabric further, and contrasted these areas with geometric patterns of whipped threads in the same bright colours. She also quilted some areas in an asymmetric pattern around shaped areas of padding to contrast with the crisp lines of the triangles and trapezoid shapes. All of the threads and colours were chosen deliberately to complement and enhance the shine of the fabric, and to represent the strong pure colours seen when light shines through glass.

Originally, Pat had planned to interpret the design in appliqué and fabric painting, enhanced by machine embroidery, but she was not happy with the trial pieces that she had worked in this way and so decided to combine hand and machine embroidery. She outlined the main shapes with machine embroidery and then worked the filling stitches and whipping, finishing off with the hand embroidery.

The back of the bag echoes the shapes of the front, but with different textures and lines in the embroidery.

These drawings show some of the different stages that the design of the bag flap passed through before its final resolution. Pat finished the flap with a handmade closure around a toning ceramic button.

JEWEL JACKET

Designed by Catrin Ann Richards

The inspiration for this jacket came from the Byzantine Empire, and is echoed in the design's rich jewel shapes and colours which are highlighted with bands of gold. The simplicity of the jacket's classic line complements the ornateness of its decoration.

The embroidery is a simple form of cutwork, or reverse appliqué. Catrin Ann tacked three layers of taffeta together, traced the design on to the wrong side, then machine-stitched through all of the layers, working on the wrong side of the fabric throughout. When the machining was finished, she cut away the layers to different depths in certain areas to reveal jewel-shaped areas of brightly coloured fabrics. To complete the effect, she made up her own buttons by cutting the shanks off some individual glass 'precious stone' buttons and mounting them in groups of different colours and shapes on to large plain gold buttons.

This jacket is part of a collection that Catrin Ann designed as a fashion student. The drawings on the opposite page show several of the other items in the range, plus the samples that she worked for each design. She prefers to work by making samples rather than by doing working drawings, as, like many textile designers, she has found that nothing compares with actually working with the materials themselves.

PUTTING ON THE GLITZ

Designed by Adele Dargue

Adele is currently studying for a master's degree in knitted textiles. This ornate jacket is part of a collection that she designed for her first degree, and it was put on show at the Conran Design Museum in London at the end of her course.

Before beginning to design any collection, Adele spends time looking for inspiration. For the shapes of the garments, she usually chooses a shape that is typical of a certain country, or of a period costume, or even of an architectural style. Then, she concentrates on finding inspiration for the colours and patterns. Once she has decided upon these, she begins to work on actual samples.

'I find that producing samples is much more important than rough drawing work. When I have done some samples, I decide how the finished effect would be used on a garment, for example, how big the design should be and how many repeats or patterns would fit across or down. It is important to get this aspect right. Then, when I have a selection of designs and samples, I choose which I should like to make up.'

Adele always uses hand embroidery on her garments, incorporating beads, sequins, sequin dust, fancy yarns, lurex, and other unusual and glittery fabrics.

Other designs from Adele's collection 'Putting on the Glitz'.

nature

INSPIRATION FROM NATURE

Since time began, the natural world has probably been the greatest inspiration for artists in all fields. Painters depict landscapes and still lifes of flowers and fruit; textile designers use patterns of animals, cloud formations, or riverside scenes; woodcarvers, stonecutters, and sculptors produce patterns made from stylized leaves and stems in all kinds of different arrangements; and, last but not least, embroiderers throughout the centuries have drawn upon the natural world for an endless fund of ideas.

Within the natural world, the greatest source of inspiration must be flowers. Oriental lacquer-work depicts exotic lilies and irises; African tribal art uses flower shapes in bright, bold colours; Scandinavian artists produce stylized tulips and narcissi in their textiles and on their woodwork; and embroiderers from virtually every culture have produced their own realistic, stylized or fantastic blooms. Gardens – your own or other people's – are good places to start your hunt for inspirational flowers, but you do not need to stop there. Visit parks and public gardens, orchid and cactus houses for unusual blooms. Send away for flower, seed, and shrub catalogues. Look in travel brochures, encyclopaedias, dictionaries of ornament, and books about other crafts – you will never run out of flower shapes to embroider! Try representing the same flower in several different styles – realistic, geometric, art nouveau, semi-abstract – and then see how you can vary the effects by altering colours, sizes, and textures. If you want some new images to fire your imagination, then look out for books on plants from other parts of the world.

Of course, if you run out of ideas on flowers then there is always the rest of the natural world waiting to inspire you! Sunsets and sunrises, trees and fields, clouds and rainbows, bugs and butterflies, rivers and streams, dogs and cats, fish and feathers, country lanes and mountain ridges – any of these could supply you with a lifetime of inspiration. Look, too, at some of the traditional arts and crafts that have used different versions of natural themes. Animals and birds appear in the art of many cultures, including tribal art, European folk art, ancient Egyptian artefacts, and oriental china and porcelain. Art nouveau and other Victorian styles are full of images of plants, leaves, exotic animals, birds, and insects, and even the more geometric art deco period features certain images from the natural world, such as gazelles, sunsets, and lightning flashes.

Try exploring the more scientific side of the natural world too. It is well known that snow crystals look beautiful under the microscope, but things like sections of stems and roots, and even bacteria and viruses, can also produce wonderful abstract patterns. Aerial photography of the countryside produces patchwork-style images which lend themselves very readily to interpretation in stitchery, and the textures of things like lichen, bark, a ploughed field, a velvety leaf, or a translucent petal can spark off numerous ideas in an embroiderer's mind.

Keep a scrap-book or folder where you can store cuttings from magazines which could be inspirational. As a starting exercise, try isolating a square or circle of a photograph, perhaps a close-up of a butterfly wing or a tree-trunk, and interpreting just that small area in different kinds of stitchery. If one method works particularly well, then try extending it or working it on a larger scale. On the opposite page you will find several photographs which might start you off on this kind of exercise. In this section of the book, all of the items have been inspired in some way by the natural world. The designs include inspiration from flowers and leaves, vegetables, birds, reptiles, countryside landscapes, fruits, pot plants, and trees – and all of the items are totally different in their style and their approach.

SMOKING HAT
Designed by Joan Bilson

The original inspiration for Joan's pillbox smoking hat came from the wonderful shapes and textures of some ornamental gourds which she had grown in her garden! She worked some studies of the basic shapes in different colour schemes and textures, and finally decided upon a yellow-based scheme.

She echoed the circular designs and knobbly textures of the original gourds by printing on to the background cotton with blocks made from potatoes, using fabric paints in several different colours. The embroidered detail was added with French knots, bullion knots, Cretan stitch, running stitch, and buttonhole stitch, worked in a mixture of coton perlé, coton à broder, and stranded cottons. The embroidered design was worked in random shapes, reflecting the random textures of the gourds.

Many Victorian smoking hats had tassels at the top or down one side, so as a finishing touch Joan made her own tassel from toning threads, experimenting first with different ways of forming and finishing the tassel head.

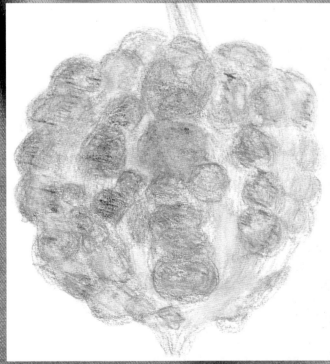

SNAKE SLIPPERS

Designed by Julia Harris

A photograph of a cobra inspired this very unusual pair of slippers, for which Julia gained a distinction in her City and Guilds (Part) embroidery exam.

Julia wanted to make the head of the cobra stand up — a challenging task! However, after several recuttings of the pattern, together with some wiring and stuffing, she finally achieved the shape that she required. For the sides of the slippers, she hand-couched a silver thread on to black polyester and interspersed it with tiny glass beads, whilst for the texture at the front she manipulated a silver fabric by stitching down pin-tucks in opposite directions.

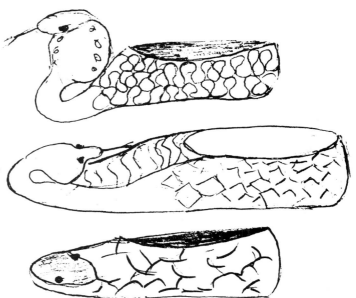

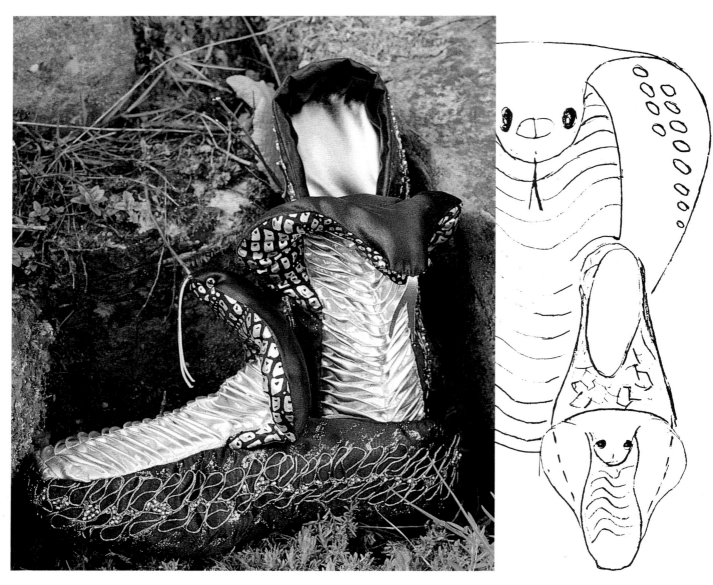

BLOOMIN' BOOTS

Designed by Lyn Griffiths

Designed especially for an Embroiderers' Guild exhibition in the Cotswolds, these boots represent the Cotswold landscape, with the soil and fields at the bottom blending into rolling hills further up.

Lyn likes to work mostly by machine. She embellished the appliquéd and silk-painted background of the boots with leaves, stems, and flowers, which she worked in wrapped string, machine embroidery on dissolvable fabric, and

quilting. She says, 'The techniques that I used for the embroidery are all ones that I use regularly in my work, so I did not need to work lots of trial pieces. However, I did stitch some sample leaves and foliage, which I later made up into a necklace. I intended these as indoor slippers for my daughter – wearable art – but I became carried away and somehow I think that they are now more art than wearable!'

PEACOCK TAIL CRAVAT

Designed by Janina Evans

As part of her City and Guilds (Part 2) course, Janina explored the subject of the peacock, tracing the use of its form in art, embroidery, and other crafts throughout history. Once she had built up a portfolio of reference material, she took the subject further by doodling and designing, exploring shapes and colours, and trying to capture the essence of the peacock form and its glorious feathers in line and colour.

When she came to make up the cravat, Janina tried out samples of machine embroidery on different fabrics, using various threads. She particularly wanted to use some areas of a shiny, bonded nylon/jersey fabric which she had discovered in a shot copper/green colour, and it worked well for the eyes of the peacock's tail feathers. Black polyester chiffon proved the best fabric for the background, and it made a good contrast to the jade green rayon thread which she finally chose to stitch most of the design.

The cravat was machine-embroidered throughout, mostly in straight stitch but with a small amount of zigzag stitch on the eyes. Janina finished the edges with three rows of straight stitch on top of each other, then trimmed the fabric back to the stitching line with sharp scissors.

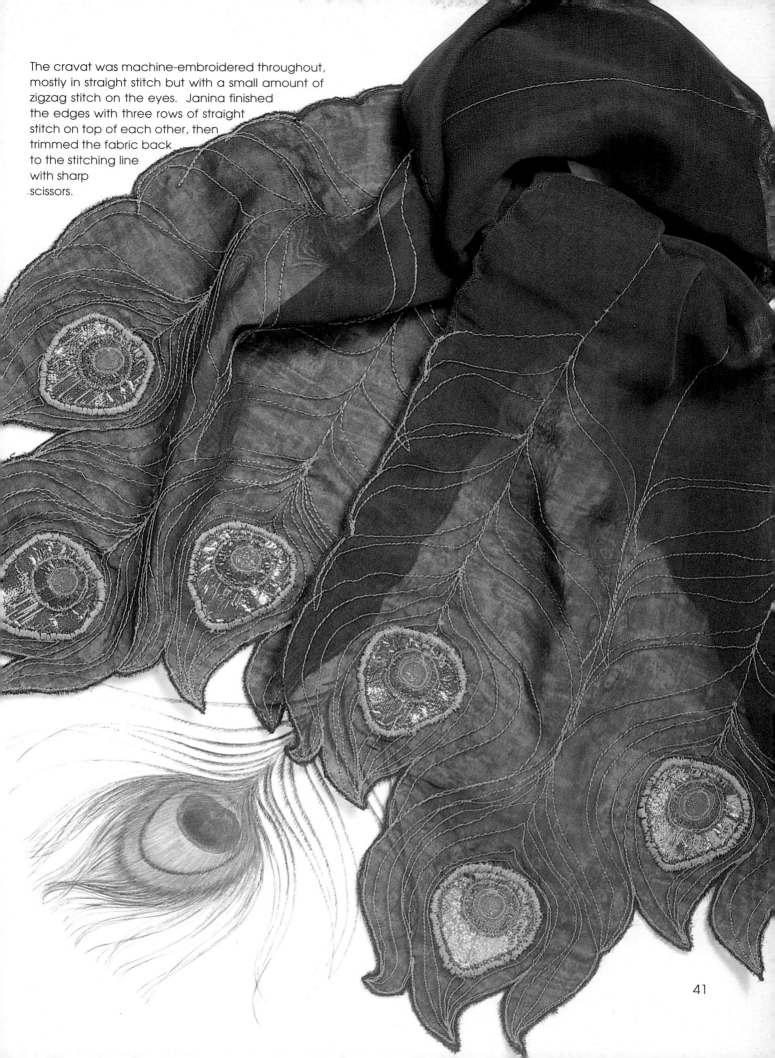

BEGONIA BLOUSE

Designed by Pamela Rooke

Pamela's design started life as one of a series of ideas for decorating a bridal gown. These explored the design possibilities of various plants and the potential of different embroidery techniques. The immediate inspiration for the blouse was a variety of *Begonia rex*. The mottled effect on the leaves suggested the idea of burning holes into a sheer fabric with the hot tip of a incense stick, which is how Pamela created the pattern!

   Originally, she worked in 'bridal' colour schemes of white and ivory, although once she had decided to work on a blouse she also experimented with steel grey and black. For the final scheme she used ivory organza and polyester satin, working the leaves in machine embroidery with white and multicoloured threads. Pamela added pearl beads to the leaves and burned in the holes before laying the organza over the satin and making up the blouse in the usual way.

SKIRT AND WAISTCOAT

Designed by Amy Lewis

Amy created this skirt and waistcoat whilst experimenting with the technique of spray dyeing. She wanted a pattern that would repeat evenly around a circular skirt and also work on the flat surface of the waistcoat, so she chose a rose and then added a simple daisy shape to create extra interest.

Amy cut out the garment pieces in the usual way, using a dressmakers' pattern. Then, she cut stencils for the daisies and a wavy stencil for the bottom line, positioned the fabric and stencils on a board to keep them flat, and sprayed on green dye with a spray diffuser. Next, she traced rose shapes on to the fabric and painted the flowers in by hand, using dilute mixtures of white and red dye for the petals, and green for the leaves. Finally, Amy pinned some very thin wadding between the fabric pieces and their linings, and quilted around each flower by hand. On the skirt, she added wadding behind the flower designs only, so that the skirt did not become too heavy. She worked in back stitch, French knots, and straight stitch, using one strand of stranded cotton for the quilting and rayon embroidery thread for the centres of the roses.

Since she made this outfit, Amy has learned to do machine embroidery and now creates a variety of free-embroidery pictures using her sewing machine.

Amy says, 'I wanted to make something pretty for my first grandchild, Helen, when she was small. I stitched this skirt and waistcoat about ten years ago, and since then it has been worn by Helen and by her younger sister Anne.'

TREE OF LIFE WEDDING DRESS

Designed by Jean Rawlinson

Jean specializes in making custom-embroidered wedding dresses. When one bride who was keen on nature and conservation came to her, Jean suggested a design based upon the tree of life. Her original inspiration came from a postcard, bought many years before at the Victoria and Albert Museum, which showed an eighteenth century tree of life embroidery. Jean used the basic colours and shapes suggested by this design, and worked out a unique variation of it for the wedding dress.

Jean made the dress itself in silk dupion, and embroidered it using a mixture of stranded cottons, silk threads, knitting yarns, and metallic embroidery threads. The embroidery included couching, satin stitch, French knots, detached chain stitch, herringbone stitch, detached buttonhole stitch, stem stitch, seeding, long-and-short stitch, chain stitch, and feather stitch.

To reflect the bride's interest in nature, the design incorporated snails, butterflies, and caterpillars on the foliage. Also, as the bride was a vegetarian, Jean added barley, peas, and other edible plants to the design. The groom's relations were Scottish and planned to wear sprigs of heather in their buttonholes, so Jean also worked beaded heather sprays into the embroidery designs for the sleeves. A final touch was the incorporation of a secret message to the bride from her mother, stitched into the back seam of the skirt!

ROSE WEDDING DRESS

Designed by Jean Rawlinson

Jean took roses as the theme for this beautiful wedding dress. The main parts of the dress are very plain, in ivory silk, with the central panels of the bodice worked in pin-tucks and stitched in gold.

Jean made the roses from the ivory fabric, which she folded, curled, and stitched into position. The leaves were made by machine cutwork. In this method, the outline of the leaf is stitched around in satin stitch or close zigzag stitch, then the shape is cut out very carefully so that the excess fabric is removed but the stitching is left intact. Jean applied the roses and leaves in an asymmetric design on the shoulders, back waist, and sleeve edges of the dress, then stitched random trails of leaves from the shoulders, down the back of the skirt, and at the waist front. The gold stitching on the leaves echoed the gold on the pin-tucks, and was picked up again in the gold shoes worn by the bride. A head-dress of matching fabric roses completed the outfit. Whenever possible, Jean likes to dress a doll in an identical outfit as a present to the bride, and this one was no exception; she made a tiny replica of the dress, including the silk rose headband, bum frill, and underskirt!

Jean continues to make wedding dresses and believes that brides are getting more daring in their requests. 'Many of the dresses have a theatrical impact, for instance, ivory silk with maroon or navy embroidery, or the dress in copper or old rose with an ivory jacket embroidered in the colour. I have even made one in a milk chocolate colour with pearls and cream embroidery!'

This picture shows the back view of the wedding dress.

WILD STRAWBERRY WEDDING DRESS

Designed by Gail Lawther

When I was looking for something a little out of the ordinary to decorate my wedding dress, I remembered a design of wild strawberry leaves, flowers, and fruit that I had worked on a baby's dress a few years before. I decided to rework it to fit my wedding dress. At that time, it was almost unheard-of for a wedding dress to have any colour on it at all, so this bold design caused quite a lot of interest. In fact, the next season it suddenly became all the rage to have touches of colour on your wedding dress – I had obviously started a trend!

As I was designing the dress itself as well, I made up a toile bodice in spare fabric to check the fit. I did not need to do this for the skirt, as it consisted simply of straight layers of gathered fabric. I chose Swiss cotton for the dress; it was a beautiful stark white with a lovely sheen. I worked the embroidery for the skirt, sash, and sleeve bands on separate strips of the fabric so that they would be more portable - at that time I was doing two long train journeys every day and could stitch whilst I travelled! The embroidery on the bodice was worked straight on to the pattern piece itself. On all of the pieces, I drew the designs free-hand and stitched them in satin stitch. The embroidery took me about six months in my spare time, and I finished the dress only two days before the wedding.

We picked up the wild strawberry theme on the invitations and the orders of service, and we had printing blocks made so that my husband, a typographer, could do the setting for the designs himself. As a final touch, our wedding cake was decorated with the same design.

Texture

INSPIRATION FROM TEXTURE

In these days of abstract embroidery, you might decide that you do not want to produce an image that is representational, but rather that you want to create a study in random line and texture. Textures surround us, but are easy to overlook if they are not on anything conventionally beautiful or 'arty'. For instance, the shapes and colours of a dry stone wall could absorb an embroiderer for years, as could a rusty gate, a piece of fancy brickwork, a delicate leaf, or even a pile of materials on a building site. Once again, the key is to look around you. Even inside your house you will discover the textures of baskets, of woods, of different fabrics and other textiles, of metal items, even of foods – think about the textures of lentils, granary bread, pasta, vegetables and chocolate!

Experiment with different ways of representing textures that are rough, smooth, shiny, uneven, patterned, wet, rasping, flabby, soft, crumbly, crisp, and undulating. Try out different combinations of threads, fabrics, and techniques to interpret your ideas, and see which are the most successful. You could use the photographs on the opposite page as starting points, then move on to more challenging textures. Look for textures in the details of photographs in magazines and newspapers; as a whole, the picture itself may not be interesting, but there may be a fascinating texture in the puddles on the pavement or in the clouds on the skyline.

One interesting way of building texture into your work is by quilting, that is, making a three-dimensional pattern by stitching into a padded layer of fabric. This texture can be altered in different ways too, by combining the quilting with fabric painting or appliqué, or by adding beads, sequins, buttons, cords, and jewels. Also, you can vary the texture enormously by altering the fabric upon which you are working: try quilting the same basic design on a sheer voile, a soft leather, a firm furnishing cotton, a metallic lamé, and a thick corduroy or denim. Then, try quilting with different stitches, by hand and by machine, or 'knot' quilting with little individual stitches or beads. Ideas for quilting designs can come from all kinds of unlikely places – railings, patterns in water, leaf shapes, rust on a car, maps, playing cards. The list is as large as your imagination! Architecture is always a good hunting ground; carvings in stone and wood, fences, columns, window frames, doorposts, floor tiles, and decorative brickwork can all produce beautiful designs for quilting.

When you are looking at texture as an inspiration for embroidery, try working a sample that reproduces the texture and colour of your original inspiration as closely as possible, and then try working a sample that uses the same texture in totally different colours and see what the effect is. Experiment with making composite patterns too. Take one small area or motif and work up simple and more complex embroidery or quilting patterns from the lines and shapes within it. These exercises will help you to see the shapes and textures around you in a new light; even the most humdrum town or village has patterns just waiting to be worked in embroidery. For extra texture, experiment with corded quilting, layered fabrics, and reverse appliqué, or try building up layers of stitching in different threads. Work the same pattern in various types of threads, from a single strand of silk to a nylon washing line, with everything in between! The different effects that these give will, in turn, suggest new ideas to you. Within this section you will find a fascinating set of items that have been inspired by textures of different kinds. These include the textures of tribal art and gold jewellery, coiled pots, pot-pourri, roof tiles, old railings, smoking jackets, and shreds of leather from a mop! The diversity is breath-taking – and so are the final results.

JEWELLERY AND SHOES

Designed by Elisabet Ehlers

Elisabet is a young and, as you can see from these pages, extremely talented designer from Sweden. The inspiration for this collection of accessories came from the theme of body decoration, in particular, tribal decorations such as body markings, symbolic tribal jewellery, and primitive signs. Elisabet's aim was to translate these markings into fabric forms, exploring traditional forms of imagery and putting them into contemporary artefacts.

She says, 'I love decoration and ornamentation. I love to manipulate and explore fabric, creating unusual concepts of decorative/sculptural forms. I have a passion for the "couture style" – the ostentatious and the lavish. The embellishment of fabric with sequins, beads, and anything sparkling, combined with a free style of embroidery, has led me to pursue the idea of sculptural forms in my work, such as unique shoe designs and embroidered jewellery. My encrusted, heavily jewelled necklaces give the illusion of reality, but in fact they are merely lightweight embroidered beads – so light that you hardly know that you are wearing them!'

Elisabet considers that her sketch-books form a very important part of her work; all of her ideas are put down on paper, either in images or words. As the next stage, she produces numerous fabric working samples, simply sitting at the sewing machine experimenting with the different textures and weights of fabrics, adding embroidery and beading to the surfaces. She uses many different techniques for the embellishments, but works all of her machine embroidery on a domestic sewing machine, removing the foot so that the needle can move more freely.

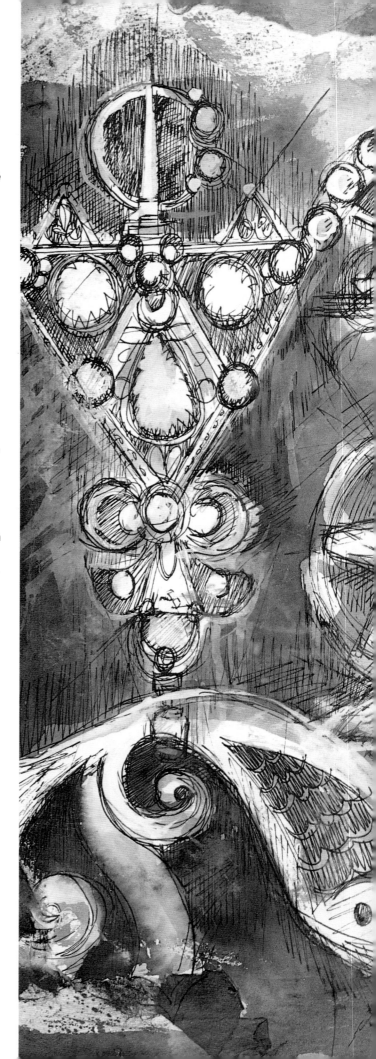

small print detail or embroidery combination for straps

shaped)

higher shaped heel

flat   pointed.

shaped both ways.

...dens for luxurious fabric / fabric to wind around the feet

to look at Tribal / primitive peoples + how they have used jewellery etc to decorate their hand and legs...

use of vivid bright colours — pay special attention to focus areas where should detail be?

straps cut out detail

Criss-cross shapes
wraps
straps
encrusted jewelled detail
printed fabric
link imagery with garments
eg. same colour scheme + linking imagery
1/4 different garments
3/4 different style shoe.

illustion of marks upon the shoe —
detail important — consider heel shape + basic style,

Fabric bulging out. textured fabric
↓ Layering / tonal cut out

straps that come up on one side

reinforce with flat wire plating.

For her shoe designs, Elisabet cuts accurate stencils for the shoe shapes, then cuts out right and left patterns in the appropriate fabrics. Whilst the fabrics are still flat, she joins any seams that are necessary, for instance, adding gold kid for the heels. Once the shapes are embroidered, she takes them to a professional shoemaker for the final construction.

POT-POURRI SHAWL

Designed by Sandra Hurll

The delicate lace shawl shown here was inspired by the colours and textures of dried hydrangea heads and also, as its name suggests, the colours and textures of pot-pourri. Sandra picked up extra inspiration by tossing together scraps of silk, lace, sheer fabrics, and silky threads to see what the effect was. Having worked several experimental and finished pieces in this kind of machine lace, she wanted to produce a light and lacy fabric that draped well. She also wanted to echo the gentle faded shades of pot-pourri and delicate Victorian colours, so she chose a colour scheme of creamy beige interspersed with subtle heather-pinks and soft greens (complementary colours) to bring the colours alive.

Sandra constructed the shawl by appliquéing fabric scraps by machine on to cold-water dissolvable fabric. She dyed some of the pieces with mixtures of dilute alcohol-based silk dyes to achieve subtle colour mixes, then appliquéd them to the background fabric using free machine stitching and a mixture of rayon, polyester, and polyester-cotton threads. Once the embroidery was complete, the background fabric, which was there purely as a support for the embroidery whilst the garment was being assembled, was dissolved by immersing the whole shawl into cold water.

For the shawl, Sandra used scraps of silk, lace, chiffon, organdie, and net, plus pieces of old lace and silk – mostly lingerie – donated by a 'magpie' friend.

The finished shawl is soft and subtle, and as Sandra says,
'It has a wonderful "memory", drapes well, and is very
flattering to wear.'

RED HAT

Designed by Mary Gillespie

Mary's coiling technique came originally from an embroidery exercise. This involved making a new fabric by joining other pieces of fabric, and then cutting up the new fabric and joining it again in a different way. Mary began cutting strips of fabric and machine-embroidering them, then rolling and coiling them into different shapes.

She says, 'Like many people, I have a collection of interesting pieces of material. I selected a piece for the red hat and started to create texture on it, using machine satin stitch and zigzag stitch over and between pieces of embroidered ribbon. From this evolved the hat, made from a mixture of flat fabric, a softly padded roll of fabric, and the embroidered cords. A rolled, embroidered ribbon and a coiled cord together formed the brooch. I was pleased with the finished result; the hat is very comfortable to wear and sits well on the head.'

PEACOCK BELT

Designed by Sue Aubertin

A final assessment for an embroidery exam presented Sue with the task of constructing a belt. During the previous year, she had been using roof tiles as an inspiration for design and texture. As you can see, she had made numerous very imaginative interpretations, re-creating the overlapping shapes in many different ways, using crayons, smocking, pleated paper, beading, layered fabrics, manipulated fabrics, and a variety of free-hand stitching techniques.

Throughout these preliminary studies, Sue kept to the terracotta, peach, cream, beige, and apricot colours of the original inspirational tiles. However, just before she started work on the final belt (see overleaf) she had a change of heart. She visited a garden where peacocks were roaming and decided to alter the colours of her construction, taking her palette from the exotic bird's tail feathers. This new colour scheme had the added advantage that it would go with many of her existing clothes.

She worked several samples to decide exactly how to construct the belt and how to work the details of the edges and fastenings. Her final method involved machine-stitching layers of metallic, satin, and net fabrics on to a stiffening fabric. Once the layers had been stitched firmly around the basic lines of the roof tile design, she tore back different areas to different depths within the tile shapes, revealing the layers beneath at random in a variation of reverse appliqué. She neatened the torn edges with machine zigzag stitch, using a multicoloured metallic thread to echo the colours and glimmer of the 'peacock' fabrics. As a final touch, she added an encrustation of beads to give a metallic gleam to the main lines of the design.

Preliminary studies for the peacock belt.

Fabric samples for the peacock belt.

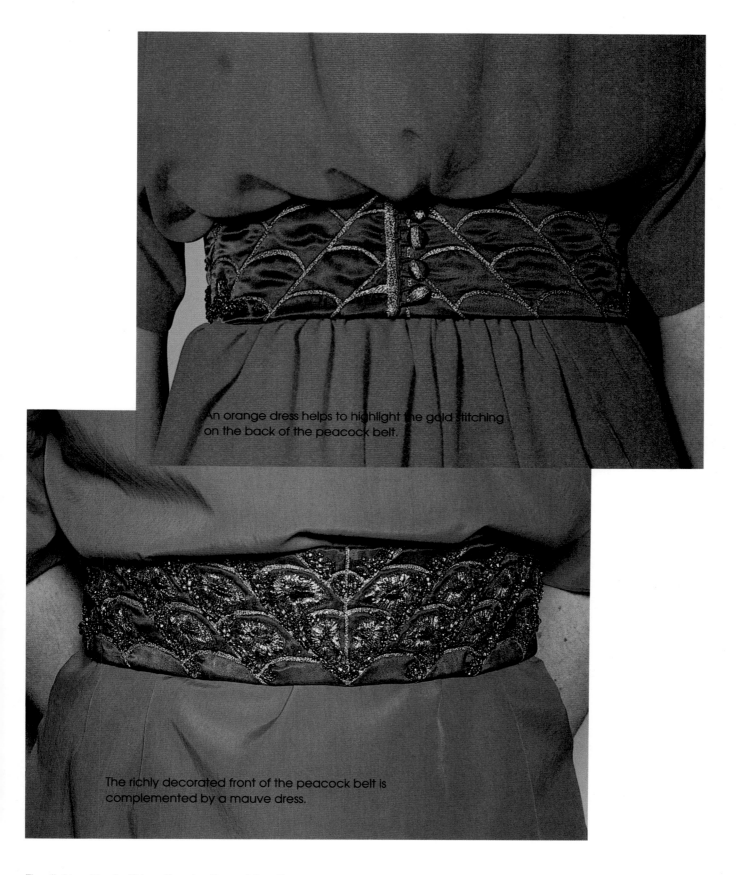

An orange dress helps to highlight the gold stitching on the back of the peacock belt.

The richly decorated front of the peacock belt is complemented by a mauve dress.

The finished belt still has the slanting grid pattern of the original terracotta tiles, but the design has been developed in a unique way to produce an eye-catching accessory based upon the beautiful colours of the peacock.

PIPED JACKET

Designed by Daphne Baker

This unusual jacket was inspired by a study of fences. Daphne chose the subject partly because of the wide variety of fencing styles within a few hundred yards of her home. She says, 'Originally, I took a photograph of an alleyway because I was attracted by the way in which some wooden palings had fallen. It was not until much later that I really noticed the dilapidated iron railings in one corner of the photograph. Once I had made a sketch, the lines suggested design possibilities, and when I had to work up some patterns suitable for a garment, I turned the original design upside-down.'

Daphne's colour scheme was governed by the colours that she finds comfortable to wear. First of all, she space-dyed some cotton in bright colours, but she was not satisfied with the result, so for the final jacket she used silk noil, damping it and applying silk paints with a sponge for the subtle shading. The quilting was worked by machine with a small zigzag stitch in silk. Daphne tried several different methods of reproducing the strong lines of the railings and finally decided upon rouleaux.

This picture shows the back view of the jacket.

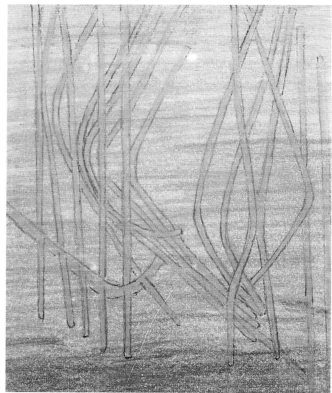

PINK AND GREY HAT

Designed by Elizabeth Gimblett

'The starting point for this piece was Greek and Egyptian statues and drawings. I wanted to use the idea of draping and pleating incorporated into a single fabric. Mariano Fortuny (1871-1949) developed this particular way of pleating fabrics so that they cling to and follow the lines of the body.'

Elizabeth chose habutai silk for this piece and dyed two lengths, one in procion brown and one in acid black with a touch of acid yellow. She stitched each length into a double rectangle, adding a line of machine zigzag stitch around the edges for extra detail. 'To pleat the fabric it is easier to have two pairs of hands! Through trial and error, I have found that the smaller the pleats the greater the finished effect. Soak the fabric

thoroughly in cold water, then pleat it widthways down its length. Once all of the fabric has been pleated, the pairs of hands should twist as hard as they can in opposite directions. Then, tie the ends together with string, wrap the fabric in foil to protect it, and bake it in a very low oven until the silk is completely dry (about four and a half hours). Unwrap the fabric. First of all, it will appear to have shrunk, but a shake will loosen the folds.'

Elizabeth made her hat shape by wrapping the fabric around her head and securing it with a steel fastener which she had made specially to complement the fabric. She is fascinated by folds of different kinds, and the inspiration for the fastener was folded paper.

BLUE WAISTCOAT

Designed by Sandra Hurll

Sandra had created a waistcoat on her previous sewing machine, using its automatic stitches on cotton ticking to explore the relationships between different lines and shapes. When she acquired a new machine, she was intrigued to try a similar experiment with it – what could it do? Would the embroidery stitches work as quilting stitches? Would the stitches work as well on silk as they had on cotton?

To begin with, she used a variety of threads and stitch combinations and produced a whole host of designs from which to choose. For the final effect, she decided to use some of the experimental techniques which had produced a richly textured fabric reminiscent of the men's waistcoats of the eighteenth and nineteenth centuries.

For the top fabric of the waistcoat, Sandra chose royal blue silk habutai, padded with a layer of 50g (2oz) polyester wadding over a muslin interlining to make the stitching easier and firmer. She used polyester thread in a matching blue and a size 80 ball-point needle so that it would pass cleanly through the delicate fabric. She found several of the features on her machine particularly useful, for instance, the pattern mirror key which produces a mirror image of the pattern. She marked and stitched the pattern pieces before she cut them out, making sure that she continued the stitched patterns well into the seam allowance so that they would not fray. For the patterns themselves, she worked out a sequence which contrasted densely stitched areas with areas of smaller stitches, lighter patterns, and plain fabric, so that all together they produced an attractive rhythm of repeats across the fabric. Once the stitching was complete, she cut out and made up the pattern in the usual way, lining the waistcoat with matching silk to hide the muslin interlining.

Detail of stitching.

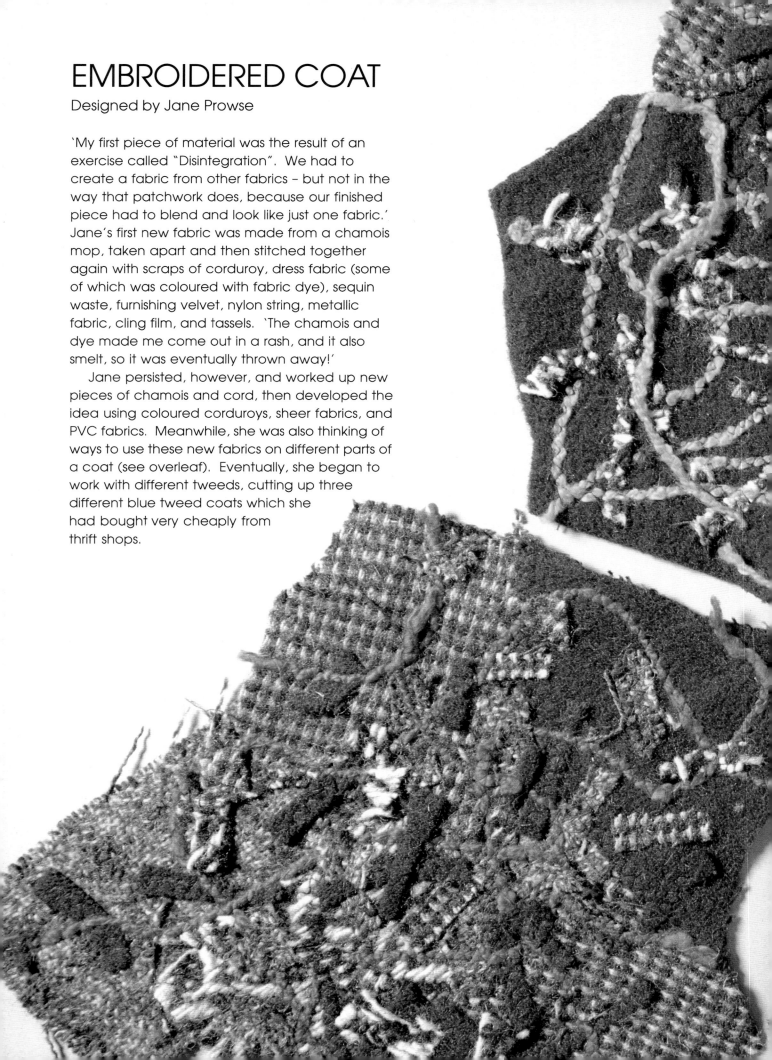

EMBROIDERED COAT

Designed by Jane Prowse

'My first piece of material was the result of an exercise called "Disintegration". We had to create a fabric from other fabrics – but not in the way that patchwork does, because our finished piece had to blend and look like just one fabric.' Jane's first new fabric was made from a chamois mop, taken apart and then stitched together again with scraps of corduroy, dress fabric (some of which was coloured with fabric dye), sequin waste, furnishing velvet, nylon string, metallic fabric, cling film, and tassels. 'The chamois and dye made me come out in a rash, and it also smelt, so it was eventually thrown away!'

Jane persisted, however, and worked up new pieces of chamois and cord, then developed the idea using coloured corduroys, sheer fabrics, and PVC fabrics. Meanwhile, she was also thinking of ways to use these new fabrics on different parts of a coat (see overleaf). Eventually, she began to work with different tweeds, cutting up three different blue tweed coats which she had bought very cheaply from thrift shops.

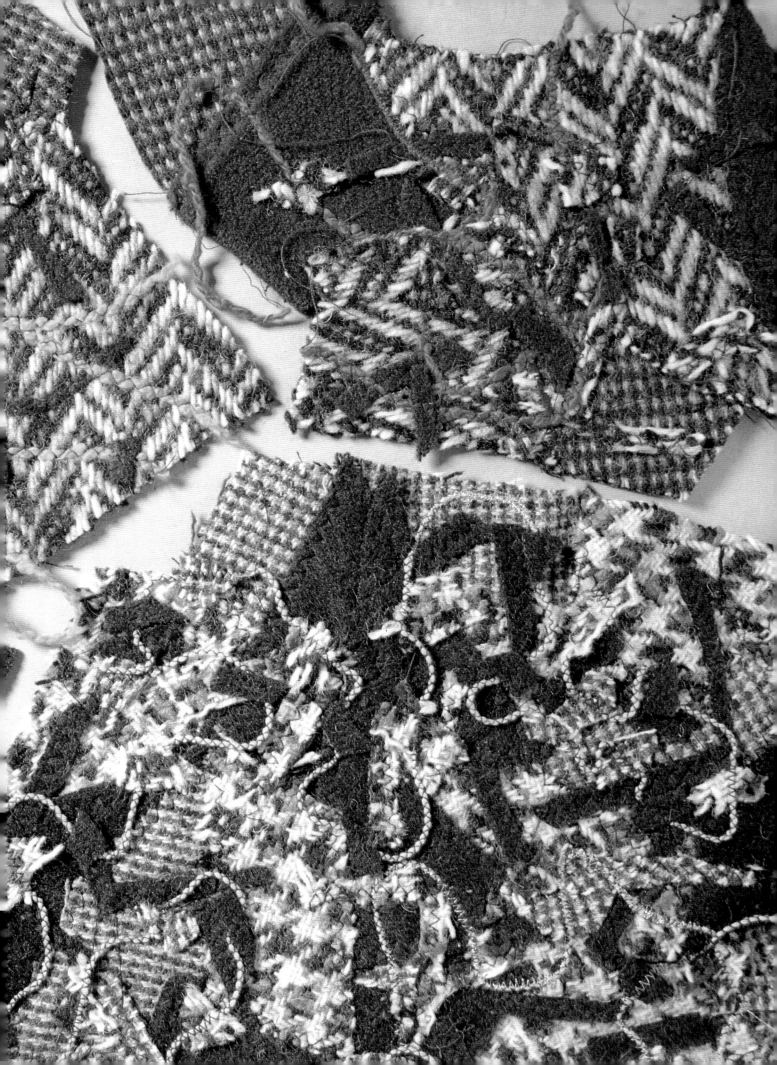

Jane's final design was applied around the top areas of a plain blue tweed coat, made by adapting a commercial pattern. 'I was looking for a cape pattern at first, because I was not sure how the garment would hang when it had the extra tweed on it, but once I saw the coat pattern I knew that it would work.'

RED JACKET

Designed by Barbara Vidal

Barbara makes many quilted jackets and her criteria are the same for each one; to make a thoroughly practical, washable, cosy jacket, in which the quilting technique enhances the structure of the design.

This particular jacket was made in red polyester satin, with the design taken simply from flowers and leaves. It is stitched by machine in polyester thread, and by hand in stranded cotton using chain stitch and French knots to enhance particular areas of the design.

Barbara feels that quilted jackets can be worked by any competent stitcher. She suggests cutting out the back of the pattern in paper (such as lining paper) first, and leaving it around on your table for a while with a pencil alongside. When inspiration strikes, you can sketch in a few lines – or rub a few out if they do not look right! The jacket back is likely to be the largest part of your design, and once you have established the design on this area, you can decide how to adapt it for the jacket fronts and sleeves. Barbara advises that you should not leave a gap of more than 5cm (2in) between the quilting lines, so that you get a fairly even quilted texture all over the garment. She works her quilting by marking the final design on to tissue paper and tacking the paper on to the sandwich of fabrics before stitching it by machine. When the stitching is complete, the tissue paper is torn away.

History

INSPIRATION FROM HISTORY

History surrounds us, and it is a great source of inspiration for embroidery! Everywhere you look you can find historical examples of motifs, textures, patterns, and shapes, not to mention concepts such as ancient tribal art, chivalry, the Garden of Eden, Greek and Roman legends, the tales of Chaucer, and the paintings of the Old Masters.

Think of all the different ways in which history manifests itself in our everyday lives. We live, work, and play in buildings which may be modern or old, and within these buildings there are design details in the brickwork, tiles, flooring, textiles, ceiling patterns, window shapes, banisters, fireplaces, covings, mouldings, door decorations, and furniture. The everyday objects that we use or have as ornaments can provide inspiration too. Look at the details on things like a silver coffee pot, an old family Bible, old photographs of relatives, or heirloom jewellery. If you look with a designer's eye, then you will see sources of inspiration in quite mundane things – the handle of an old teaspoon, an ancient heating grille on a Victorian building, a monogram on an old post-box, or a geometric design on a piece of Chinese porcelain.

Books are useful sources of historical inspiration too. There has been a vogue recently for producing facsimile editions of everything from Mrs Beeton's *Book of Household Management* to plates of early plant drawings and paintings, and these are rich in ideas for the embroiderer. Books on the history of architecture, sculpture, painting, textiles, engineering, aviation, cars, and microscopes may also spark off design ideas in your mind. Remember to look at details –

signs, decorations, borders, and textures. These can often prove to be more inspirational than the main part of the picture, for instance, in a photograph of an old steam train you might see a decorative brass handle, or in a picture of an ancient French château you might be inspired by the patterns of its formal garden.

Historical themes can be wonderful starting points for designs. For instance, you might decide to explore Aztec civilization. You could start by studying relevant books which deal with their architecture, artefacts, and lifestyle. Then, make sketches of designs, patterns, details, and shapes, and see what ideas these spark off. Start compiling a file of ideas that seem relevant, such as cuttings from magazines that conjure up an image of Aztecs in your mind, or fabrics and yarns that seem to have the right feel. Next, begin to experiment with your ideas on fabric – try different hand and machine embroidery techniques, different stitch textures, different mixtures of fabrics and different ways of manipulating or combining them. To start you off, the photographs on the opposite page may give you some ideas. The items in this section have all been inspired in different ways by historical subjects. Scottish castles, Egyptian jewellery, traditional Japanese stitchery, and the arts and crafts of ancient Turkey are some of the subjects that have been used as spring-boards for the beautiful finished items, which vary from belts to jackets and from collars to cuffs. Feast your eyes upon this section, then look around you and see how different historical ideas could be spring-boards for your own creativity.

TURKISH JACKET

Designed by Pat Elkington

The inspiration for Pat's jacket came from a study of Turkish designs. She looked at everything Turkish, from kelims and carpets to ceramics and calligraphy, and made extensive notes and sketches. Her City and Guilds project brief called for a constructed item, and an exhibition at Liberty's turned her thoughts to making an embroidered garment. Quilted jackets were very popular that particular season, so she opted for the design idea that she thought would work best in that medium. She worked on silk because, she says, ' I love it – it takes dye so beautifully, and its sheen makes it very rewarding for quilting. I was trying to produce a sumptuous jewelled effect of rich colour and decoration, echoing the sensuous curves and ornate patterns of Islamic designs. Also, I had just been given some industrial machine-embroidery threads in a range of muted metallic colours, which I wanted to exploit.'

Pat tried various methods of producing the patterns. Embroidering motifs and applying them separately was too lumpy, and she felt that applied machine lace was too fragile for a jacket, so finally she decided upon fabric painting for the main outlines. She dyed the background fabric with cold-water dyes, and painted on the motifs with a permanent gold paint. Then, she embellished the surface with machine straight stitch, satin stitch, pattern stitch, and whip-stitch, and added a few French knots by hand.

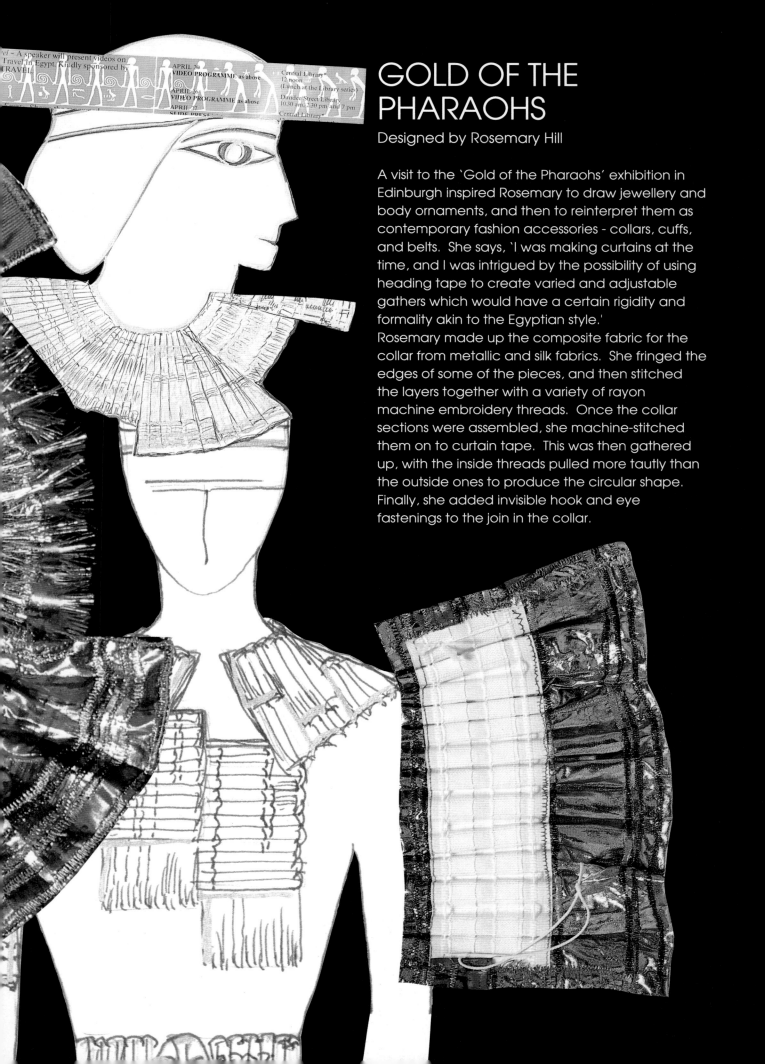

GOLD OF THE PHARAOHS

Designed by Rosemary Hill

A visit to the 'Gold of the Pharaohs' exhibition in Edinburgh inspired Rosemary to draw jewellery and body ornaments, and then to reinterpret them as contemporary fashion accessories - collars, cuffs, and belts. She says, 'I was making curtains at the time, and I was intrigued by the possibility of using heading tape to create varied and adjustable gathers which would have a certain rigidity and formality akin to the Egyptian style.'

Rosemary made up the composite fabric for the collar from metallic and silk fabrics. She fringed the edges of some of the pieces, and then stitched the layers together with a variety of rayon machine embroidery threads. Once the collar sections were assembled, she machine-stitched them on to curtain tape. This was then gathered up, with the inside threads pulled more tautly than the outside ones to produce the circular shape. Finally, she added invisible hook and eye fastenings to the join in the collar.

EGYPTIAN JEWELLERY

Designed by Sandra Avril Kendrick

Not surprisingly, the art and jewellery of ancient Egypt were the inspiration for Sandra's set of 'body jewellery', which consists of a collar, cuffs, and belt (see overleaf for the finished items).

Sandra started by compiling an extensive notebook featuring all kinds of Egyptian influences, and then experimented with various ways of producing an Egyptian feel with fabric and embroidery. For the items themselves, she finally settled upon the idea of trapping one layer of bright fabric behind another, transparent one.

Firstly, she dyed the basic silk fabrics with intensely coloured silk paints to create the vivid hues, then cut the silks into tiny pieces to produce a jewel-like effect, securing them to the background with an iron-on bonding fabric. Next, she put a layer of twinkle nylon, a shiny transparent fabric, over the top, and couched a grid formation in gold on top of this. Her notebook shows experiments with an irregular grid, but she eventually used an even one which radiates outward to follow the shape of the collar and cuffs. Silk and metallic gold threads were used for the machine embroidery.

'The technique of trapping small pieces of fabric between layers was a new concept to me, and I thoroughly enjoyed it – although I have not used it since! This is mainly because with City and Guilds embroidery one always tends to move on to new pastures. I now do a great deal of smocking, both traditional and contemporary, and I also like shadow work.'

Pages from Sandra's notebook.

Stylised form of the Scarab Beetle.

Top.

Bottom.

Necklace using gold disks,
Carnelian, Lapis lazuli,
Turquoise, Obsidian and
green Calcite.

silk, coloured
in of gold
turquoise
beg.

To fasten her collar and belt,
Sandra made use of that most
Egyptian of symbols, the sacred scarab beetle.

MULTI-PURPOSE SCARF

Designed by Elizabeth Porter

Elizabeth's scarf is an unusual garment that can be worn in many ways. It can be put around the neck of a white blouse to act as a collar or scarf, used as a headscarf in several different styles, or worn around the waist as an apron-style belt.

Like Rosemary Hill's collar, pictured on pages 82-3, Elizabeth's inspiration was 'The Gold of the Pharaohs', and she has used many different techniques to add gold details to the basic triangle formed by the white cotton background fabric. She appliquéd gold leather and lamé, made use of beading and fabric painting, and also machine-embroidered shapes which she worked on water-soluble fabric and then applied to the basic fabric. To maintain the golden theme, Elizabeth used gold and variegated metallic threads for all of the embroidery. She finished the scarf by fringing and knotting the edges, adding gold beads at intervals.

The final garment can be used for both day and evening wear, giving totally different effects depending upon the way that it is worn and the garment with which it is worn.

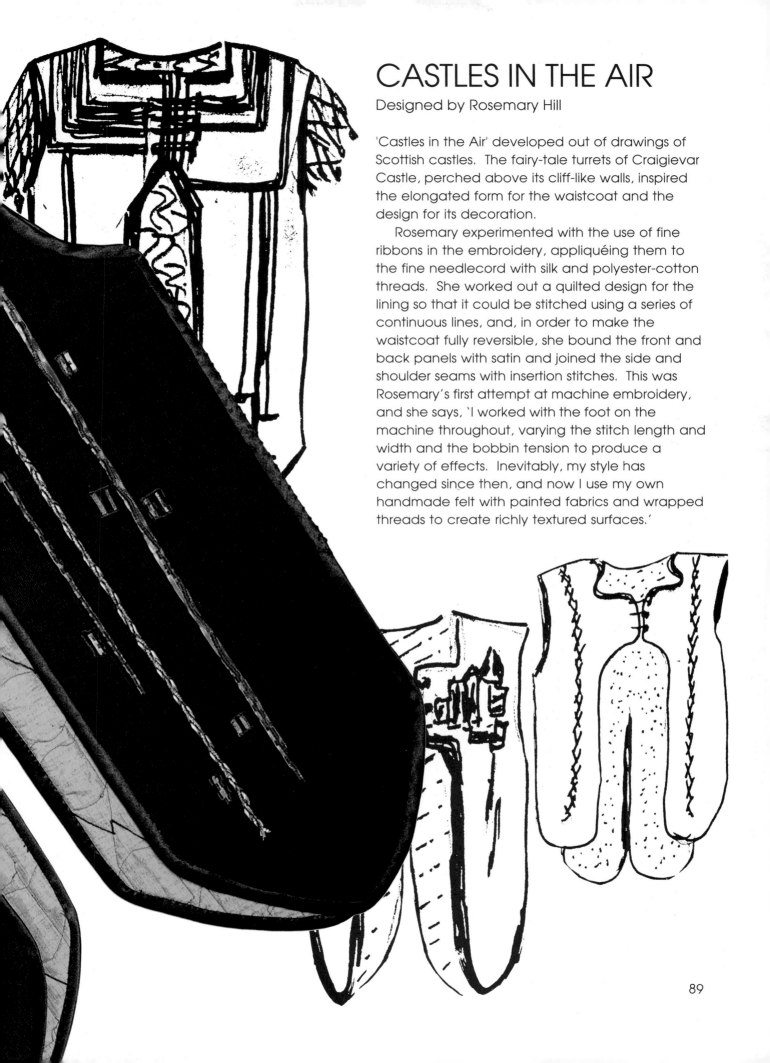

CASTLES IN THE AIR
Designed by Rosemary Hill

'Castles in the Air' developed out of drawings of Scottish castles. The fairy-tale turrets of Craigievar Castle, perched above its cliff-like walls, inspired the elongated form for the waistcoat and the design for its decoration.

Rosemary experimented with the use of fine ribbons in the embroidery, appliquéing them to the fine needlecord with silk and polyester-cotton threads. She worked out a quilted design for the lining so that it could be stitched using a series of continuous lines, and, in order to make the waistcoat fully reversible, she bound the front and back panels with satin and joined the side and shoulder seams with insertion stitches. This was Rosemary's first attempt at machine embroidery, and she says, 'I worked with the foot on the machine throughout, varying the stitch length and width and the bobbin tension to produce a variety of effects. Inevitably, my style has changed since then, and now I use my own handmade felt with painted fabrics and wrapped threads to create richly textured surfaces.'

SOLAR COLLAR
Designed by Cam Duncker

Cam made a study of collars from the eleventh century onwards and was fascinated by the way in which collars were depicted as symbols of wealth, power, and status. Having looked at a number of historical portraits which showed elaborate collars in great detail, she decided to create a double collar. One layer could be worn on its own, or the two could be put together for a grander occasion. The primary collar was based upon the great shells worn by Pacific peoples, whilst the secondary, asymmetric collar was designed to be worn either as a deep yoke to frame the inner collar or as a ruff behind the head.

To embroider the double collar, Cam used a wide variety of goldwork materials and hand stitchery, plus some machine embroidery which she worked over lightly padded silk.

91

The thick walls
of rubble & [...

Che[...

impost
from whi
ch springs]

PENDRAGON BELT

Designed by Carol Newman

When Carol began her City and Guilds embroidery course, she was terrified of producing a sketch-book. 'I hated the idea of drawing in public, and for weeks I carried it about and could not draw a thing. Eventually, the rucksack and I went to Glastonbury, because I am hooked on King Arthur, and I sat under a huge tree on a scorching day and drew the Abbey ruins. Because it was too hot to move, I made a large number of sketches!'

The shapes of the Norman arches appealed to Carol, so she carried out some research at her local library and also – having finally got over the 'coyness barrier' – made more drawings at Canterbury and Winchester. For her exam assessment, she chose to make a belt inspired by the chevron arch decoration. She worked several experimental pieces, but felt that these first trials were disappointing. Thinking about words associated with King Arthur, Carol came up with a list: tough, noble, royal soldier, Celtic, and primitive. She translated these words into fabrics, and the ideas became silk, velvet, and coarse evenweaves, in royal colours of red, blue, purple, and black.

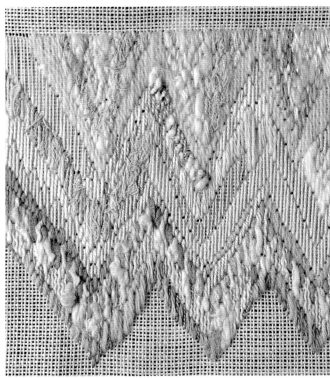

For the belt itself, Carol machine-stitched a random appliqué of roughly cut fabrics, then cut away layers in chevron shapes to reveal the fabrics beneath. She embroidered long straight stitches to emphasize the chevron shapes, and finally added some Russian braid as an edging plus a few antique buttons from her secret hoard!

SASHIKO JACKET

Designed by Margaret Blakeley

Several unusual techniques are combined in Margaret's jacket. Over the past few years she has become very interested in Sashiko quilting, a Japanese method of quilting fabric with decorative running stitches. The fabric is sometimes padded slightly, but often, as with this jacket, the technique is simply worked on two layers of fabric placed together. The stitching is designed to show and takes the form of long running stitches worked in a variety of geometric patterns.

In this simple jacket shape, Margaret has echoed the lines of the traditional Japanese kimono, with its straight wide sleeves and asymmetric areas of stitched pattern. On each area of stitching she has used a different pattern. The coloured borders provide contrast to the grey background fabric and are worked in Seminole patchwork. This method involves strip-piecing fabrics, cutting them into shapes, and then reassembling them at different angles to produce patterns. In Margaret's jacket, the strip-pieced fabrics were embroidered with various machine-stitched patterns before being cut up and reassembled.

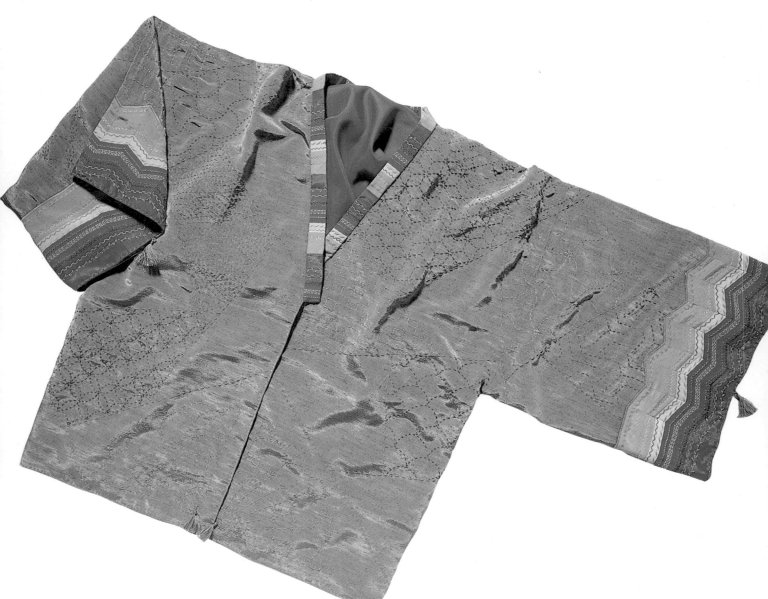

INDEX